Isaac Newton

Discovering Laws That Govern the Universe

Michael White

BLACKBIRCH PRESS, INC.

WOODBRIDGE, CONNECTICUT

Published by Blackbirch Press, Inc.
260 Amity Road
Woodbridge, CT 06525
web site: http://www.blackbirch.com
e-mail: staff@blackbirch.com

First published in Great Britain by Exley Publications Ltd., Chalk Hill, Watford, 1991.
© Exley Publications Ltd.
© Michael White

10 9 8 7 6 5 4 3 2

Photo Credits

Ann Ronan Picture Library: 38; Bridgeman Art Library: 15, 16, 28, 59; by permission of the British Library: 31 (left); by permission of the Syndics of Cambridge University Library: 43; E T Archive: 11; Exley Publications: 33; Lincolnshire County Council: 12, 14, 34; The Mansell Collection: 20, 54; Mary Evans Picture Library: 7, 13, 25; Michael Holford Photographs: 37 (below), 52–53 53 (below); Millbrook House Ltd. (P.B. Whitehouse): 48 (above); The Museum of London: 26–27; NASA: 30, 31 (right); National Trust Photographic Library/Tessa Musgrave: 45; Paul Brierly: 22, 44; PSA Photo Services: 56–57; Royal Society (photograph by Professor Roy Bishop, Acadia University, Nova Scotia, Canada): 13 (above); Scala: 41; Science Photo Library; 4 (NASA), 5 (Mikki Rain), 9 (Alexander Tsiaras), 18 (David Parker), 36 (NOAO), 37 (Dr. John Lorre); ZEFA: 8, 48 (below), 49. Cover: Art Resource

Printed in China

Library of Congress Cataloging-in-Publication Data

White, Michael, 1959–
    Isaac Newton: discovering laws that govern the universe / by Michael White.
        p. cm.—(Giants of Science)
    Includes bibliographical references and index.
    Summary: Describes the life and scientific contributions of the famed English mathematician who changed our perception of the universe.
    ISBN 1-56711-326-5
    1. Newton, Isaac, Sir, 1642–1727—Juvenile literature. 2. Physics—History—Juvenile literature. 3. Physicists—Great Britain—Biography—Juvenile literature. [1. Newton, Isaac, Sir, 1642–1727. 2. Physicists.] I. Title. II. Series.
QC16.N7W44 1999
530'.092—dc21
[b]

98–49142
CIP
AC

Contents

The Problem of Gravity

In the summer of 1666, a young man strolled into the orchard of his mother's house in Woolsthorpe, Lincolnshire, in England and sat down beneath a tree to concentrate on his studies.

A moment later, an apple fell and landed on the young man's head. The·young man was twenty-two-year-old Isaac Newton. No doubt it hurt for a moment, but it also started the young scientist thinking about the properties of moving objects.

Isaac had already struggled to understand what kept the Moon in its orbit around Earth, and the planets in their courses around the Sun. It was only after he had thought about why the apple had fallen to Earth, that he really began to answer these questions. The answers, he found out, lie in the theory of gravity.

"The Miraculous Year"

For Isaac Newton, 1666 had been an astonishing year. Only weeks earlier, the Great Fire of London had swept away the last remnants of the plague, which had taken thousands of lives. Newton was a student at Cambridge University, but he had to

Opposite: *The calculations needed to successfully complete the 500,000 mile round trip to the Moon are based on the law of gravity discovered by Isaac Newton.*

Below: *An artist's impression of the moment an apple fell on Newton's head.*

5

stay with his mother in the countryside for more than a year because Cambridge was ravaged by the highly contagious disease. In the countryside, Newton could enjoy solitude and relative safety. In this peaceful setting, he could concentrate on the scientific problems that he had been grappling with throughout his post-graduate years.

During the past year, Newton had made incredible breakthroughs in mathematics and physics. In 1665, he had found the answer to a problem that had eluded the most gifted mathematicians for years—the binomial theorem.

A while later, Isaac began to work on what was to be the greatest development in the history of mathematics—calculus. Today, scientists use both of these theorems in computer programs. Space engineers use calculus and the binomial theorem to help solve complex mathematical problems. Economists use these branches of mathematics to predict what will happen to all the various currencies around the world.

Isaac Newton was a mathematical genius who, by his early twenties, had studied the work of every notable mathematician in the world. Then, when he had exhausted all current knowledge, he began developing his own theorems and methods to create a mathematical foundation for his scientific work. When he became famous, writers looked back on this short period in the Lincolnshire countryside and called it "The Miraculous Year."

Newton's World

In the seventeenth century, when science was in its infancy, many well-educated people still believed in witchcraft. Little was known about the fundamental principles behind the way many things worked. Most people thought the universe was

6

controlled by an all-powerful deity, and many events and phenomena were caused by spirits. There were no solid theories of mechanics or ideas about how things moved. Scientists knew very little about light and how it behaves, and subjects like chemistry and medicine were based more on magic than science. Nobody really understood how the planets and Moon were kept in their orbits, or why it was that falling apples always fell toward the ground. Yet, by the end of Isaac Newton's life, he would have the answer to all of these things. His answers would revolutionize the scientific process and would completely change the way people looked at the world.

The work Newton began in "The Miraculous Year" would be the basis of mathematics and physics for the next 300 years. Within three centuries of that apple landing on his head, scientists

Isaac Newton was born into a society where few people knew anything of science, and explained even the simplest phenomena as resulting from witchcraft, spirits, and demons. In this picture, an old woman is being arrested as a suspected witch.

Expert billiard players need years of practice to estimate forces and angles needed to get balls into pockets. Using Newton's laws of motion, it would be possible for a computer to be programmed to be a world-champion billiard player.

would land on the Moon and send machines to distant planets using his theorems and discoveries. Whole areas of physics and mathematics are called "Newtonian," in honor of his outstanding accomplishments.

The Versatile Scientist

Newton's laws of motion explain how forces act upon objects, whether moving or stationary. By applying these laws to any mechanical system, it is possible to predict the effect a force will have on an object. If, for example, the weight and force of two pool balls are known, by applying Newton's laws, the affect one ball will have on the other can be predicted. Today, Newton's laws of motion are used in all areas of science—designing cars, planning the course of a spaceship, building aircraft

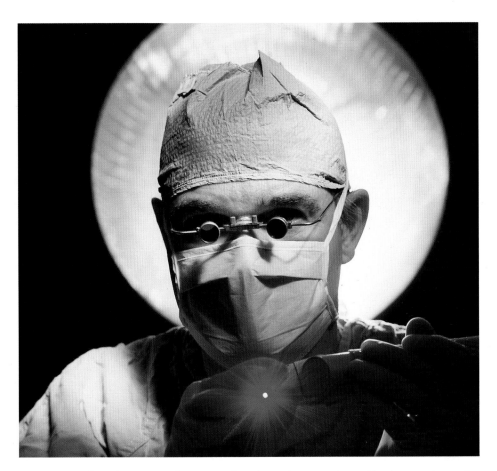

engines, and making aerodynamic skateboards. In addition, Newton worked out a theory of gravity to explain how the planets travel in their orbits around the Sun. The same theory also explains why we remain held firmly to Earth, and do not all float off into space.

Newton also worked in many other areas of physics. His groundbreaking theories on light have helped scientists and engineers design better telescopes, microscopes, eyeglasses, and cameras. His discoveries in optics ultimately led to inventions such as televisions and lasers.

The story of how Isaac Newton came to make these monumental discoveries began in Lincolnshire, where he was born. From such simple origins, his influence eventually spread to change the world.

Isaac Newton made great discoveries in the study of light, which has helped in creating twentieth-century technology. Here a surgeon uses a laser during an eye operation.

Childhood in Lincolnshire

Isaac Newton was born just after midnight on Christmas Day in 1642. He was premature, and the doctor who attended his birth did not expect him to survive. His father, a fairly prosperous farmer, had died three months earlier, leaving Isaac's mother, Hannah, to raise the tiny boy on her own.

During this time, England was in a state of tremendous upheaval. In 1629, King Charles I had dissolved Parliament because he wanted to rule the country without having to abide by set laws.

Charles I reigned in this way for eleven years, with his opposition growing continuously. Throughout the country, people were angered by the introduction of new rules for the Church of England, and the unpopular King's unlawful demand of money.

The year Newton was born, a civil war broke out to determine who would hold the power in the land—the king or Parliament. Several bloody battles followed between the Parliamentarians and the Royalists, led by King Charles I. Isaac was just six years old when England's civil war ended. This division of the country would affect England throughout his life.

Most of Lincolnshire was in the hands of the Parliamentarians, but Isaac's family supported the king. The only way they could survive was to keep their Royalist views to themselves.

The Hated Stepfather

Isaac's mother remarried when he was three years old. His stepfather was a wealthy clergyman, Barnabas Smith, who was rector in the village of South Witham a few miles away from Woolsthorpe. Smith ordered Hannah to leave her son with his grandmother at Woolsthorpe and move to South Witham to look after her new family. Isaac told close friends many years later that he felt only jealousy and hatred for his step-parent.

Isaac never got along with his grandmother. Friends and colleagues rarely heard him speak of her. Some people have said that the trauma he experienced over his mother's second marriage accounted for his melancholy as a teenager and his well-known depression later in life.

When Isaac grew older, he began to keep a diary in which he poured out his feeling of hatred for Barnabas Smith. Almost eighty years later, he would tell friends how he often dreamt of killing his step-father and rescuing his mother from the "beast."

A Fascination with Machines

Isaac's childhood was a lonely time—he made few friends and kept to himself. Often he would lock himself in a room at his grandmother's house and spend the day making models, kites, sundials, and little mechanical devices.

Before long, young Isaac became well known in the district for his creations. Local people and relatives were amazed by his skill at constructing exact replicas of carts and wheeled machines. When he was thirteen years old, he built a scale model of a new windmill in the village. It worked perfectly. He even managed to set the sails in motion by placing a mouse on a wheel inside.

Throughout his life, Isaac used his natural talent as a craftsman to build models and to make scientific instruments. He used one of his creations, a reflecting telescope, in his famous experiments with light.

School Days

When Isaac was ten, his stepfather died and his mother returned to the house at Woolsthorpe. Two

The English civil war had begun shortly before Isaac's birth, and raged until he was six. King Charles I was executed in 1649.

11

years later, the boy went to Grantham grammar school nearby, where he stayed with his uncle who lived in town.

He was considered only average by his teachers and antisocial by his classmates. He admitted later that he ignored his work, and spent most of his time making models and carrying out his own experiments.

Isaac was unpopular with the other boys. He was physically weak as a child and could not take part in rough games that were a part of daily life at school. He was a serious, quiet lad who rushed home to his tiny room to make his models and furniture for doll houses. Instead of being impressed by his skill, the other boys were jealous of his ingenuity and scientific talent.

One day, Isaac got into a fight with a school bully. The bully was much bigger, and extremely unpopular with the other boys. Despite being small and quite frail, Isaac won the fight by clever manipulation. He wound up giving his rival a severe nosebleed. After his victory, Isaac was admired for his clever thinking. His newfound popularity encouraged him to work harder in school. Before long, he became an intellectual leader, gaining the respect of his teachers and classmates.

Farmer or Scholar?

Despite Isaac's success, Hannah Newton decided to take her son away from Grantham grammar school so he could work on the family farm. If it were not for some remarkable twist of fate, Isaac may have remained a farmer for the rest of his life. First, his great genius had already been recognized by two very important people—his uncle and the headmaster of Grantham, Henry Stokes. During his last few years at school, Isaac had become the

Isaac Newton at age twelve. This portrait successfully captures the thoughtfulness and melancholy of the young Newton.

Above: *Woolsthorpe Manor, the house where Isaac Newton was born.*

Left: *A scene from a typical classroom in a seventeenth century school.*

Isaac carved his name on a window ledge at Grantham School. Years later, when he had become a world-famous scientist, they preserved the inscription for the amusement of future generations.

star pupil. The headmaster considered Isaac to be the best student he had ever taught. The boy was always reading scholarly books and devising ingenious solutions to problems. He worked on the theories of early scientists, finding answers to intriguing mathematical puzzles and scientific curiosities. But, despite his intellectual skill at school, Isaac was absentminded and forgetful—often leaving the chores on the farm unfinished.

Because of this, his mother decided that the young man would not make a good farmer, and reconsidered his future on the farm.

After much persuasion, and at the insistence of the two influential men in his life, the eighteen-year-old Isaac was admitted to the prestigous Cambridge University.

Isaac's mother was not poor, but she could not afford to support her son at the university. For extra money, Isaac would have to become a "sub-sizar." This meant that he earned his keep by cleaning the rooms of paying scholars, serving meals, and doing menial jobs. Young Isaac forced himself to put up with these indignities because he was thrilled to be at the university. He was surrounded by other intellectuals and thinkers. And, in three short years, he would graduate and be a true scientist.

Early Days at Cambridge

Isaac arrived at Cambridge on June 4, 1661. The grand college buildings that stand alongside the river filled the young freshman with awe. Cambridge was not a large city. To anyone arriving from London, it would seem a quaint, picturesque little town. But to Isaac, who had left the quiet Lincolnshire countryside, it was a real change of pace.

He began preparing for his studies right away. On the first day he purchased a lock for his desk, a bottle of ink, a notebook, and a pound of candles, which he would use to light his room as he worked through the evenings.

Isaac's enthusiasm, however, was soon dampened when he realized that he had not really moved from the rough, boyish life of school. Many of the other students were just like the boys he thought he had left in Woolsthorpe. As a strict Protestant, his religion forbade him to spend a lot of time drinking and gambling. At the university, Newton was confronted with such things for the first time. After forgoing these activities, he soon gained a reputation for being a boring, solemn young man.

Eventually, things settled down and Isaac found a friend—fellow Protestant student John Wickins. The two friends shared a room at Trinity College, Cambridge.

After a few months at the university, Isaac began to relax and enjoy student life. He did not desert his faith, but he started to enjoy an occasional visit to the tavern with John and a game of cards with his friends.

The Wren Library at Trinity College, at about the time Newton was a student at Cambridge University.

New Ideas

It was at this time in his room at Cambridge that Isaac began to formulate his early theories on force and movement. He started to develop his ideas about the nature of light, and later, figured out how a specially shaped piece of glass, called a prism, can split light into a rainbow from red to violet. He also began to think more about gravity. Before he went too far, he had to understand the principles underlying the subjects he pondered. To do this, Newton knew that he would have to use very advanced mathematics—he would have to learn everything he could about each subject. And, although he did not realize it then, he would have

15

to invent his own system of mathematics—a system that he would call calculus. In addition, he had to continue his other college work and pass his exams in order to stay at Cambridge, which was no easy accomplishment.

Opposite: *It would have been in taverns such as the one shown here that Isaac and his roommate, John Wickins, would have the occasional ale and enjoy a game of cards with other friends from the university.*

A Lucky Find

One Sunday in 1664, Isaac visited a fair in Cambridge. Among the sideshows and novelty stalls, an object sparkled in the afternoon sun. It was a prism. He was struck by its beauty and fascinated by the smoothness of its surface. He realized that he could carry out some useful experiments with the prism, so he bought it. Back in his room at Trinity, he began to experiment with it that very afternoon.

The Rainbow Effect

First, he pulled the curtains across all but one window. Over the remaining window he placed a piece of cardboard. He had cut a tiny slit in the cardboard so that light could filter into the room from the bright sunshine outside. Then, he stood back and watched the narrow beam of light entering the dark room. Next, holding the prism up to the light, he let the beam enter one side of the prism and observed the different bands emerging from it. The natural light that had entered the prism was split like a rainbow. It ranged from violet at the top through indigo, blue, green, yellow, and orange, with red right at the bottom.

Isaac was fascinated. People had seen this phenomena many times before, but no one had really investigated what caused it. Many believed that the rainbow effect was already contained within the prism and was released by shining sunlight on it. Scientists of the day realized that the glass was altering the light that entered the prism, but they did not know why.

. . . .

"According to my own observation, tho' Sir Isaac was of a very serious and compos'd frame of mind, yet I have often seen him laugh, and that upon moderate occasions. . . . He usd a good many sayings, bordering on joke and wit. In company he behavd very agreably; courteous, affable, he was easily made to smile, if not to laugh. . . . He could be very agreable in company, and even sometime talkative."

W. Stukeley, Newton's first biographer

. . . .

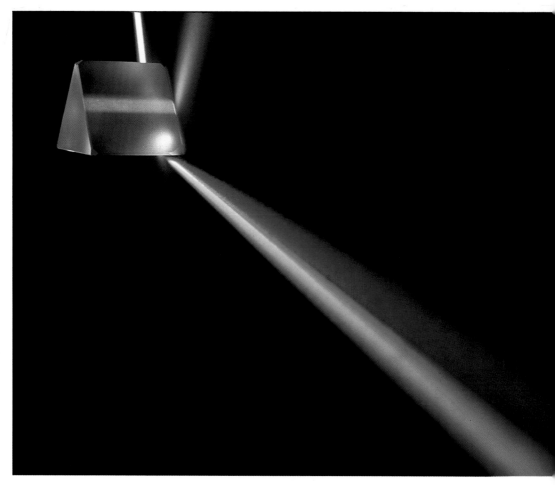

In his first experiment on light, Newton discovered that when white light is shone through a prism it splits into a rainbow, which he called the spectrum. The light ranges from violet at the top to red at the bottom.

More Experiments

After he had produced the rainbow on his wall—what he called a spectrum—Isaac set about experimenting with what he had observed. First, using a piece of cardboard with a narrow slit in it, he blocked off all the different bands coming out of the prism, except the red one. Then, he sat back and looked at the single red band on the wall and wondered what to do next. What would happen, he thought, if he passed this red beam through another prism? Would this then split into a rainbow just as the sunlight through his window had done?

He purchased another prism and placed it in the path of the red band of light. He turned to see what emerged from the other side. Coming from the far side of the prism was nothing more than the same red beam he had shone through it. All that happened was that the beam was a little bent from the path it had taken through the glass.

This could only mean one thing. Sunlight contained all different shades of the spectrum—violet, indigo, blue, green, yellow, orange, and red—and that was that. It was impossible to keep dividing light further.

The First Modern Scientist

It is amazing that nobody had discovered these properties of light before. Because prisms were considered to be toys, scientists never bothered to experiment with them.

Isaac recorded his findings and thought about what it all meant. He measured the width of each band, changed the distance of the prism from the wall, and tested all of the possibilities. Then, he put his findings into a mathematical language.

This was typical of Isaac Newton. Not content with simply making observations, he always translated what he saw into a mathematical language. From there, he came up with general theories. This ability to take a discovery from observation to development of theory is what made him so different from other scientists at the time.

Isaac spent many months at Cambridge working with his prisms, devising more experiments. At times, he would work nonstop. On more than one occasion, John Wickins found him sprawled out over papers on his desk, having fallen asleep struggling with a difficult problem. He often forgot his meals, and his cat grew fat eating the untouched food that was constantly left on the edge of his desk.

After many experiments, Isaac realized that our eyes see objects because the light all around us

19

reflects, or bounces off, whatever we are looking at. As it reflects, the light arrives at "sensors" in our eyes that translate and send the information to our brains. Based on his experiments, Isaac had discovered that visible light, the light that enables us to see the objects in our world, is made up of all the different shades of the rainbow. When these are mixed, we see white light. When one part of the spectrum is missing, the light no longer appears white—it becomes tinted.

Many scientists would have stopped there, but Isaac always worked on a problem until he felt there was nothing left to learn from it. Having established that light was made up of different shades of the spectrum, he wanted to see if he could recombine them to make white light again.

He set up his piece of cardboard in the window and allowed some light to pass through the slit. This light passed into the prism just as it had done in the first experiment. The color spectrum appeared on the wall. This time, instead of blocking off all but the red band, he let all the light from the first prism pass into his second prism, placed close to the first. A single beam of white light emerged from the glass of the second prism. He was probably the first person in history to bring together all of the shades of the rainbow into a single beam of white light. He had actually made and then unmade a rainbow!

The Spinning Circle

Isaac performed one more experiment, just to make sure his amazing findings would be believed. He realized early on that the spectrum was not made up of equal amounts of each shade—in a rainbow there is always more blue than red. So, he simulated, or copied, the way nature mixes the colors of a rainbow.

Opposite: *Newton became fascinated with the properties of the prism and conducted many experiments with it in his room at Trinity College.*

. . . .

"I never knew him to take any recreation or pastime either in riding out to take the air, walking, bowling, or any other excercise whatever, thinking all hours lost that was not spent in his studies."

Dr. Humphry Newton,
Isaac Newton's assistant

. . . .

He made a small circle of cardboard about four inches (10 centimeters) across and divided it into seven different-sized sectors. These sectors represented the seven visible bands of the rainbow, which he then painted with the spectrum's colors. Next, he mounted the cardboard circle on a spindle and spun it around quickly.

Staring at the spinning object from a distance, it looked white! Because the circle was spinning so quickly, the different shades in their correct proportions appeared to merge and looked white.

A Clearer View

Isaac did not publish his work right away, so most of his discoveries with light were not read until many years later. But even then, other scientists were quick to take advantage of them.

In the seventeenth century, eyeglasses were a rarity only worn by the wealthy. Even so, they were of remarkably poor quality. Within a few decades of publication, Newton's findings helped scientists to produce great improvements in the design of lenses and the manufacture of eyeglasses.

The microscope had been invented more than fifty years before Newton's birth, but it was relatively primitive device that produced only a fuzzy, blurred image. By the eighteenth century, application of Newton's discoveries had turned it into a far more sophisticated instrument. This, in turn, led to breakthroughs in many areas of medicine and biology.

Probably the most important result of Newton's work with light during those months in Cambridge was the eventual creation of a whole new science—spectroscopy—which developed a hundred years later. Spectroscopy is the study of the light that is emitted by flames when a material is burned. The flames seem to have many different reds, purples, and blues jumping among them. The reason for this is that when different materials are burned, they produce light made up of different amounts of each of the shades of the spectrum. By allowing this light to pass through a prism, scientists can split the light into its component parts, exactly as Newton had done with sunlight. Then, they can discover what chemicals are in the material that is being burned.

Flight from the Great Plague

Isaac made all his great discoveries with light before he graduated from Cambridge. In April 1664, after three years' study, he became a scholar of the college. He was elevated from the position of subsizar, and no longer had to perform menial duties. A year later, in 1665, he received a

"His breakfast consisted only of bread and butter and a tea made by boiling a bit of orange peel in water which he sweetened with sugar. He partook freely of wine only with dinner, and for the most part drank only water."

W. Stukeley, Newton's first biographer

Bachelor of Arts degree, which was automatically awarded after four years at the university. This meant that he could spend four more years living at Trinity College, pursuing whatever areas of knowledge he wished to study.

Isaac continued to develop his ideas about how light worked. At the same time, he began researching the properties of gravity and how the planets move in their orbits.

His early experiments at Cambridge, however, were interrupted. A terrible disease was spreading through England, devastating families and communities everywhere. The Great Plague began in London, where people lived in cramped, unsanitary conditions. Victims had terrible fevers and their bodies were covered with huge running sores. If one caught the plague, death was certain. The corpses were collected and transported through the city in great wagons. Then they were buried in mass graves away from the main population. In some of the worst-hit districts, the dead and dying outnumbered the living.

Then, during the hot months of 1665, the plague began to spread beyond the capital. People going outside London carried the dreadful disease to other cities and began to infect other populations. By June 1665, fear of the plague caused Cambridge to close its doors. Isaac moved back to Lincolnshire, where he could continue with his studies at the manor house.

Back Home

During his last year at Trinity, Isaac had been working especially hard.

Although the study of mathematics was an important part of his work, there were very few mathematicians in the world who had developed anything like the techniques he needed. But there

were some, and he managed to track down their books in the great libraries at Cambridge.

Isaac found works by Rene Descartes, and the British philosopher Henry More. These men were leaders of the "New Science," a bold and imaginative movement of thinkers throughout Europe, who were trying to expand the frontiers of modern science and mathematics.

At Cambridge, in early 1665, Isaac read everything he could by these great thinkers. When he

The Great Plague of 1665 was one of the worst natural disasters in the history of England. The terrible disease eventually struck down more than a million people.

The Great Fire of London began on September 2, 1666, just before the plague had completely died down. It started in the heart of London and spread to engulf the entire city for four days.

could not find what he needed to further his early theories, he created his own mathematics.

By the time the plague made Cambridge too dangerous, he had taken the first few steps toward solving the problems inherent in developing his theories. The peace and solitude of Lincolnshire served to nurture his inventive mood.

In late summer, the great breakthrough came. When the apple tree incident occurred, Isaac began to formulate his theory of gravitation.

Gravity

At Cambridge, Isaac had been toying with the idea that some forces of nature act from a distance. The idea that one object could affect another without being connected by wires or strings was a strange concept at the time—one that very few scientists had imagined before. But the evidence was growing that there was indeed such a force—the force that kept the planets in their paths, for instance. There was definitely some attraction between objects that was invisible to the eye. How else, Newton stated, could the planets stay orbiting around the Sun? And the Moon orbiting Earth? There were no strings holding Earth and the Moon together, so how could these things happen unless some unknown, unseen force was at work?

When the famous apple fell from the tree in Lincolnshire, Isaac knew that it had been pulled to Earth by the same invisible force that kept the planets and the Moon in their orbits—the force of gravity. Earth was exerting a pulling force on the apple, which dragged it down. Isaac reasoned that it was the same force the Sun exerts on the planets. But, if that was the case, why did the planets not crash into the Sun?

The Pail of Water

Isaac struggled with his questions about gravity for days. Then, just as he was packing to return to the university, the truth struck him. For some strange reason, at that very moment, he remembered a game the children played at school. They would each take turns standing in the middle of the playground, holding a rope that was tied to the handle of a pail of water. The idea was to spin around the pail of water at the end of the rope as fast as you could. To win, you had to whirl the pail of water around your head without spilling a drop. Everyone was astonished at how the water always stayed in the pail as it spun around.

Suddenly it all made sense. Planets don't crash into the Sun because of their sideways speed—the speed they have as they orbit. As for the pail of water, the tension of the rope pulling inward forced the pail to travel in a circle, but the water was obeying what was later to become Newton's First Law of Motion. The object naturally moved in a straight line and it, therefore, remained in the pail. By the

Rene Descartes was probably the greatest French scientist and philosopher of the seventeenth century. Descartes' writings represented the basic ideas of the "New Science," which laid the foundations for Isaac's monumental work.

Newton's Law of Gravitation

All bodies in the universe attract each other with a force that is directly proportional to the product of the masses of the bodies and inversely proportional to the square of the distance between them.

same token, the apple had fallen straight down to Earth because it had no sideways speed or velocity.

Back to Cambridge

By 1667, the plague had subsided and Cambridge was deemed safe again. The university re-opened, and in March, Isaac returned to his room in Trinity College.

When he had settled in, he began to work on the gravity theory he had conceived just before leaving Lincolnshire. True to his nature, he wrote out a mathematical formula to see if his idea could work. After weeks of concentrated effort, he had completed his calculations. By studying his outcomes he saw that he was indeed correct. There was an invisible force at work that held the planets on their predictable courses.

Not satisfied with this breakthrough, he wanted to know more about gravity. He realized that this force must get weaker the further away each object was from the other. He knew, for instance, that planets furthest away from the Sun must experience a weaker pull than those closest to the Sun. But how did the strength change?

Using the advanced mathematics he had developed before leaving Cambridge, he worked out a formula that showed how gravity force weakens with distance. If one planet was twice as far away from the Sun as another, the formula said, then it

"After dinner, the weather being warm, we went into the garden and drank tea, under the shade of some apple trees, only he (Newton) and myself. Amidst other discourse, he told me, he was just in the same situation, as when formerly, the notion of gravitation came into his mind. It was occasion'd by the fall of an apple, as he sat in a contemplative mood. Why should that apple always descend perpendicularly to the ground, thought he to himself."

W. Stukeley, Isaac Newton's first biographer

NASA astronaut Edward White floats above Earth. In orbit, objects (including humans) experience weightlessness because there is almost no gravity in space.

felt only a quarter of the force of gravity. If it was three times further away, it felt only one ninth of the force.

After working with his calculations, Isaac instantly realized what the outcome of his formula must mean. If his numbers were right, the force of

gravity obeyed "an inverse square law"—in other words, if the distance between objects was doubled, the force of attraction between them was a quarter of what it was before. If the distance was tripled, the force was one ninth. If the distance apart was four times greater, the force was one sixteenth the original strength.

Fellowship

The discovery of the various laws of gravity was a tremendous breakthrough. Scientists before him had imagined such an invisible force in nature, but

Above left: *An eighteenth-century cartoon lampooning Newton's theory of gravity.*

Above: *The Space Shuttle* Atlantis *lifting off from the Kennedy Space Center. The voyage of a spaceship relies on extremely accurate calculations. Newton's theory of gravitation is used almost in its original form in order to program them.*

nobody had managed to find out how it worked or
how its strength changed at different distances.

Isaac's discoveries with gravity and light, along
with his new mathematics, won him instant recognition and election to the illustrious position of
Fellow of Trinity College. All this happened to him
within six months of returning to Cambridge
University, at the age of twenty-five.

It was a meteoric rise, made possible in part, by
his growing friendship with Trinity's Professor of
Mathematics, Isaac Barrow. The two Isaacs made
an odd pair. Barrow was an extrovert and popular
with everyone. Newton was shy and withdrawn.
Barrow realized Newton's potential after seeing the
work he had done during the plague years, but it
was the publication of a new work by a Danish
mathematician, Nicolas Mercator, that brought
Newton's genius to the attention of the rest of the
scientific world.

In 1668, Mercator published a book of mathematics called *Logarithmotechnia*. A few weeks after
it was published, Isaac received a copy and began
to read it. Within a couple of hours he was panic-
stricken. Mercator was writing about the very
same mathematics he, Isaac Newton, had discovered years before the plague. Isaac had recorded
his findings, but he had not published the results.
The only person who knew that he had been first
with the discovery was Professor Barrow.

Most people would have immediately publicized
the fact that they had made the discoveries three
years before. But, in some ways Isaac Newton was
a peculiar man. He was always cautious, even
secretive, about letting other people see his work,
and this attitude remained with him into his old
age. If it wasn't for the fact that his pride would not
allow him to remain silent, he may never have got-
ten credit for any of his mathematical discoveries.

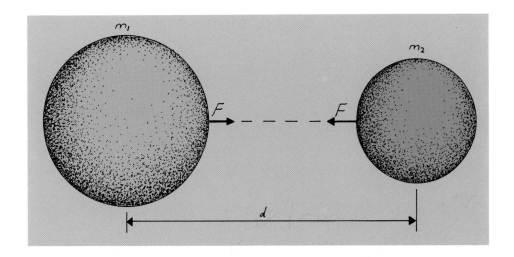

Newton's Plan

Isaac asked Professor Barrow to publish his original manuscript anonymously and to circulate it among his powerful colleagues in London and Europe. Only when this paper was accepted as the original breakthrough would Barrow be allowed to announce the author's name.

Within two days, Isaac had the original manuscript cleaned up. Professor Barrow saw that it was circulated. In this first published work, Isaac explained his ideas in far greater detail than the mathematician Mercator had done in his book. After a few weeks, the whole scientific community had accepted this version of the story. It was only then that Isaac Newton became renowned for his mathematical breakthrough.

Professor of Mathematics

Not long after his first publication, his friend and great supporter Professor Barrow decided to retire to pursue his private studies. He nominated his favorite colleague as his successor. At the age of twenty-six, Isaac Newton became the youngest professor of mathematics ever to teach at Cambridge.

Above: *This diagram illustrated Newton's law of gravity. The force of attraction between their bodies depends upon the mass and the distance between them. This is represented by the equation F=G m m/d2, where G is the power of gravity, m and m are the masses of the bodies and d is the distance between them.*

Being given a professorship was a major achievement, especially for one so young. Isaac Newton was an undisputed brillance. But, Isaac was not a genius at everything. The job as professor required that he deliver lectures a few times a year, which was difficult because he was a poor speaker. The attendances gradually fell, and, on one famous occasion, he gave a lecture to an empty room, with only the walls as an audience!

In all other respects, the post suited him perfectly. It paid a reasonable salary and he only had to do a little teaching and attend occasional meetings and ceremonies. Most importantly, it gave him the freedom to develop and pursue his own studies.

Galileo's Refracting Telescope

The first telescope had been invented in 1608, more than sixty years before Isaac Newton began using one. Although he did not invent the device, the great Italian scientist, Galileo Galilei, improved the design and made the instrument popular around 1610.

Galileo knew that light moved in straight lines. He also realized that when light from a distant object arrives at the surface of a lens, it is bent by the glass of the lens. So, if an observer placed an eye on the other side of a "bulging" or convex lens, the light arriving at the eye appears to come from a much bigger object.

Galileo's device, a refracting telescope, consisted of two lenses placed at either end of a tube. The lens at the far end of the tube was called the object lens and the one near the eye was called the eye lens. The object lens focused light into the tube and the eye lens magnified the distant object by bending the light coming from it.

This type of telescope worked very well. Within a few years, refracting telescopes were used by

"Sir Isaac in mathematics could sometimes see almost by intuition, even without demonstration. . . ."

William Whiston

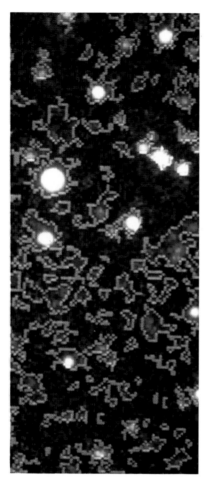

astronomers all over Europe to study the Moon, the stars, and the planets of the solar system.

A New Type of Telescope

·In the early 1670s, Isaac built a new, more powerful type of telescope. It consisted of a mirror placed at one end of a thick tube. The mirror was a special type—a concave mirror—which is curved. Look at it from the front, it curves inward.

Isaac realized that if light from a distant object, such as a planet, hit this special mirror it would bounce back to a point in front of it. The mirror produced the same effect as the eye lens in a refracting telescope. It made the light appear to come from a much closer object. If the light was then reflected into an eyepiece at the side of the tube, the observer would see a magnified image of the planet. Isaac called his telescope a reflecting telescope.

Isaac's amazing new telescope was revolutionary (and he made it with his own hands). He had ground the lenses, shaped and polished the mirror, and built the tube. He had even designed and made his own tools!

The Royal Society

Isaac Newton's reflecting telescope was an instant sensation, and other great scientists of the day realized that they had a true genius in their midst. In early 1672, he was invited to join the distinguished Royal Society.

The Royal Society was a small circle of senior scientists who had formed themselves into a group in 1660, when Isaac was only eighteen. They had the support of King Charles II, and among the membership were such important and famous men as the chemist, Robert Boyle, and the scientist and architect who built London's St. Paul's

Opposite below: *The telescope that Newton designed in the 1670s.*

Above and opposite above: *Galaxies millions of light years away from Earth. The development of sophisticated telescopes, based on Newton's principles, have enabled astronomers to see further into space than ever before.*

Cathedral, Christopher Wren. An invitation to join their ranks was a great privilege. Isaac jumped at the chance.

Disagreements

Soon after joining the Royal Society, thirty-year-old Isaac Newton delivered his first paper. This involved demonstrating one of his theories, accompanied by a short publication. Newton spoke about his theory of light and the spectrum. He also met another great scientist, Robert Hooke, who would later become secretary of the Royal Society.

The two men were both highly respected scientists and great personalities, but they approached science in totally different ways. They never saw eye to eye.

Isaac was always very careful and meticulous. He persisted with a problem until he had the answer. Hooke was an excellent scientist who worked on many different problems at once. He did not, however, explore each problem in as much depth as Isaac Newton did.

Hooke considered himself to be the expert on light. He disagreed with Newton's theory and championed his own ideas. For the first time in his life, Isaac was confronted with a scientific equal. For many years the debates raged at the Royal Society and in the scientific community at large. From that very first meeting, the two men could never be friends—and they were often enemies.

A meeting of the Royal Society during the time of Newton's presidency. He is in the middle of the picture, chairing the proceedings.

Alchemy

Back in Cambridge, Isaac carried on with his studies in private.

Because of all the arguments and squabbling at the Royal Society, he decided to leave physics and mathematics for a while. Instead, he began to devote his time to furthering his studies in other areas of science. For many years, the subject that occupied his thoughts most was alchemy (the forerunner of chemistry).

Alchemists were not scientists. They were more like magicians, intent on achieving the impossible (making potions to produce immortality, love potions, and magical cures). Isaac would not have liked to be known as an alchemist. They kept few records of their discoveries and did not really understand what they were doing. Isaac only got involved with such things because he had an endless thirst for knowledge. He wanted to know everything, and any area of study interested him.

He could see that many amateurs who were working on alchemy were going about things in a terribly disorganized way. Isaac was convinced he could make a valuable contribution to this largely unexplored area of science.

The Careful Scientist

Always meticulous and careful, Isaac recorded his discoveries in alchemy and backed up all his ideas with experiments.

Many people consider Isaac Newton to be the first "real scientist" because of his very careful and disciplined methods, and because he used mathematics to describe the things he could observe and prove from experiment.

Isaac used his methods in alchemy, but unlike his work in physics and mathematics, he made no great breakthroughs. Day after day, he would sit in

"What is important for Newton, he recognized his own capacity because he understood the significance of his achievements. He did not merely measure himself against the standard of Restoration Cambridge; he measured himself against the leaders of European science whose books he read."

Richard Westfall, from his biography, *Never at Rest*

. . . .

"Caution, prudence and reserve were natural elements in Newton's character. Any natural tendency to exuberance in him were, like the slightest leaning towards convivial dissipation, soon outgrown. Springing from the lowest stratum of the landed gentry, his father unable to sign his name, Newton had met with little family understanding of his own intellectual interests: it is always less easy to live with genius than to admire it posthumously."

Rupert Hall

. . . .

his self-built laboratory at Trinity. He had constructed his own array of bottles and tubes, beakers and condensers, and devised experiment after experiment. But, he had little luck. The secrets of chemistry would always elude him, and after many years of research he achieved little.

Then, one warm June evening in 1679, news came that altered the course of his life and brought an end to his alchemical studies. Newton received word that his mother Hannah was very ill. He returned home to Lincolnshire immediately.

Back in Lincolnshire

For the next six months, Newton could not think of alchemy, or even his beloved physics and mathematics. All of his time was occupied with sorting out the affairs of his mother's estate. Apart from a younger half-brother, Benjamin Smith, the son of his hated stepfather, Isaac was the only heir.

It took many months to sort out the maintenance of the manor and the adjoining farmland. Benjamin was an unreliable youth and could not be trusted to run the estate. To make things worse, the young man was ill and bedridden, and Isaac had to organize nursemaids. It was not until the beginning of 1680 that he was able to hand the estate over to a worthy manager and to return to scholarship and his experiments at Trinity.

A Return to Mechanics

Returning to Cambridge, Isaac decided to put aside his alchemical experiments for a while. In London, arguments with Robert Hooke were becoming increasingly bitter. Isaac tried not to lose his temper in public. For most of the next few years, angry letters continued to pass between Hooke in London and Newton in Cambridge. Hooke was forever stating that the theories on

which he and Isaac agreed were ones he had thought up first. This was to be the case with the laws of motion, which Isaac was working on.

On one occasion, when Hooke claimed that he had discovered one of Newton's theories first, Isaac wrote to the Secretary of the Royal Society:

"Hooke has done nothing and yet written in such a way as if he knew and had sufficiently hinted all but what remained to be determined by the drudgery of calculations and observations, excusing himself from that labour by reason of his other business: whereas he should rather have excused himself by reason of his inability."

The two scientists very rarely met, except at Royal Society meetings, and even then there was usually a frosty silence between them.

One good thing did come from this rivalry. Isaac became so angry with Hooke's constant statements about being the first to discover his theories of motion, that the Cambridge man threw himself even more completely into his research.

Despite his pride and anger, Isaac still found it difficult to allow his work to be published. Even though his friends were constantly pushing him to share his discoveries with the world, Isaac always claimed that he was not ready. It seemed as if nothing would change his mind, until his closest friend decided to intervene.

A Persuasive Friend

In May 1684, Isaac's most trusted friend, the scientist Edmund Halley, made a special trip to Cambridge. His mission was to persuade Newton to publish the results of his work on mechanics (the science of how objects moved), which he had been developing off and on since the Great Plague.

At first, Isaac was not convinced. He was not prepared to publish anything half-hearted or unfinished.

. . . .

"Newton . . . was obsessed with the ideal of rigor and could hardly convince himself that anything was ready for publication."

Richard Westfall, from his biography *Never at Rest*

. . . .

Halley suggested that Newton should not simply publish a small booklet of half-finished ideas. Halley offered to finance the publication of a book describing all the ideas he knew his friend had formulated. He also convinced Isaac that, unless he moved quickly, others may beat him to it and there could be a repeat of the Mercator episode from sixteen years earlier.

Edmund Halley left Cambridge with Isaac's assurance that he would devote himself entirely to writing a full account of his greatest discoveries.

The Pinnacle of Scientific Achievement

It took Isaac only eighteen months to finish his book, working night and day to complete it. He hardly slept, and ate only when his hunger was so great that he could no longer concentrate.

Once an experiment was devised, Newton would repeat it many times in order to eliminate errors or any possibility of chance. He then kept impeccable records of his findings.

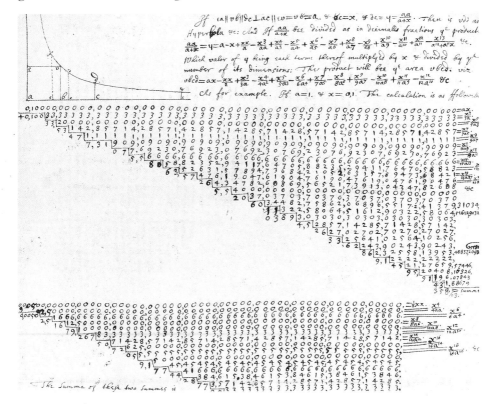

Newton's laws of motion in action. Here you can see the balls of a toy, called Newton's Cradle, colliding as they go through a periodic swing. The motion of the balls demonstrates the laws Newton encapsulated in his famous work, the Principia..

On April 28, 1686, the masterpiece was finally ready. It was called *Philosophiae Naturalis Principia Mathematica*, but is usually referred to as the *Principia* (The Principles). It was delivered to the Royal Society that evening and excerpts were read to the gathered scientists, although the author himself decided not to attend.

To most of the scientists, the book was a revelation. It described Newton's ideas of gravity, the centrifugal force, and how the two are related. In addition to these older ideas, there were plenty of new proposals. Most importantly, however, the *Principia* contained what became known as Newton's laws of motion.

Inertia

There are three laws of motion stated in the *Principia*, but the first, which deals with the concept of inertia, has the widest applications.

Inertia is the term given to the tendency for all objects to resist change or movement. In order to move an object, a force has to be applied to overcome its inertia.

Newton stated that because of their inertia, all things remain in a state of rest, or moving in a straight line, unless affected by an outside force.

It is easy to see that this must be true. If a perfectly smooth ball was rolled along a perfectly smooth surface, and there was no wind or any other force at work, the ball could, in theory, carry on rolling forever. Of course, in real life the ball would slow down and eventually stop, and that is caused by outside forces, such as friction and air currents.

Isaac Newton's immediate predecessor in the field of mechanics was the great Italian physicist Galileo Galilei. He had studied the properties of

The Principia *has been described as the greatest scientific work of all time. It was an immediate success within the scientific community throughout Europe and Newton became accepted as Britain's greatest scientific genius.*

Newton's Laws of Motion

1. *Every body continues in a state of rest or uniform motion in a straight line unless it is acted on by an external force.*

2. *When a force acts on a body, the rate of change of momentum of the body is proportional to the force and changes in the direction in which the force acts.*

3. *To every action there is an equal and opposite reaction.*

falling objects, but no one before Newton had thought about—or undertaken experiments to see—why a force had to be applied to a stationary object in order to make it move.

New Wisdom

Today, such notions as force and inertia are scientific "givens." In Newton's time, however, the notion of forces and the application of energy to overcome inertia was a totally new idea.

A thousand years before Newton's time, the Greek philosopher, Leucippus, had proposed the theory of causality. He had written that "nothing happens without a cause, but everything with a cause and by necessity."

This seems an obvious statement, but it is very vague. Newton explained the idea that forces need to act on an object and need to overcome inertia if the object is to react. He proved this idea using geometry, and predicted the effect caused by the application of forces of various strengths on different objects. This is where Newton's "real" science was so different from the philosophies of the

"Isaac Newton's work *Principia Mathematica*, which he wrote in only eighteen months, was published in 1687. It embodied all his works on mechanics and is considered by many to be the greatest scientific work ever produced."

James Carvell, from *Famous Names in Engineering*

Greeks and the pseudo-scientists up to Galileo's time in the early an mid 1600s.

Newton laid down laws that could be applied to predict events with remarkable accuracy. Newton's theory of mechanics was systematic, it was built on sound fundamental principles and simple, irrefutable laws that could be applied to the most elaborate and complex problems (problems such as sending spaceships to the planets, or something as relatively simple as the movements of a billiard ball on a smooth surface).

The most revolutionary aspect of Newton's discoveries was the idea that an object moves or changes course because of external forces acting upon it—and not due to a consequence of an internal change within the object itself. A jet aircraft moves by obeying Newton's Third Law, "For every action, there is an equal and opposite reaction." A force thrusts combustion gases backwards out of the engines while an equal and opposite force pushes the aircraft forward.

A Practical Concept

Within a few years of the publication of the *Principia*, the idea of inertia, along with the consequences of the other two laws, had started to transform the world for other scientists and engineers. These people incorporated Newton's laws into designs for machines and scientific equipment, clocks, and wheeled devices, anything that involved moving parts. In most cases, Newton's laws made it possible to work out whether a machine would function properly before it was even built.

Isaac Newton had laid the foundation for a whole new era of scientific invention, eventually paving the way for the great industrial revolution. It was his laws of motion that made it possible for

"So intent, so serious upon his studies that he ate very sparingly, nay, ofttimes he has forgot to eat at all, so that, going into his chamber, I have found his mess untouched, of which, when I have reminded him, he would reply—"Have I!" and then making to the table, would eat a bit or two standing, for I cannot say I ever saw him sit at table by himself. . . ."

Dr. Humphrey Newton, Isaac Newton's assistant

47

the British engineer, Isambard Kingdom Brunel, to build his enormous steamships and suspension bridges in the nineteenth century. Without Newton's laws of motion, James Watt could not have constructed the first working steam engine less than 100 years after the publication of the *Principia*. And without the steam engine, the world's rail networks would never have been built.

Opposite and above: *These pictures show everyday examples of modern engineering that rely on the laws of mechanics and dynamics expressed in the* Principia.

Modern Applications

Architects and builders also gained great knowledge from the *Principia*. Newton's laws are still the basis of modern mechanical engineering. They are used by people working in almost every field of science, from oil-well technicians to space engineers, from car designers to satellite fabricators.

When rockets travel to the Moon, they are designed to overcome the principle of inertia exactly as it was described in the *Principia*. The rocket is launched into Earth's orbit using powerful engines, but in space there is no friction or air to slow it down. So, engineers at mission control simply fire a tiny booster engine on the side of the ship, called a retro rocket. This sets the spaceship's course to the Moon. Because all objects continue moving in a straight line until affected by an outside force, the rocket just keeps going until it reaches the Moon. After that initial burn, no more thrust is needed. It is so easy to move in space that the rocket would crash into the Moon if it was not slowed down by another booster, thrusting in the opposite direction as it approached the surface.

Isaac Newton's *Principia* achieved nothing less than describing the laws of motion that govern the universe. It has been acknowledged by many to be the pinnacle of scientific achievement, the greatest work of science in history.

There was one man, however, who did share the world's enthusiasm for Newton's Principia—Robert Hooke.

Hooke attacked Isaac over the contents of the *Principia*. Hooke claimed that Newton had stolen his ideas of gravity and that he, Robert Hooke, had devised the inverse square law of gravity, (which was the central pillar of Newton's work).

Each rival had his followers at the Royal Society (and in the rest of the scientific community of Europe). After months of fierce arguments in letters and various debates among colleagues, Isaac finally won when Robert Hooke's suggestions were discredited by most of his peers in the scientific community.

The Black Years

For many years after the publication of the *Principia*, there was a silence from the room at Trinity. Isaac busied himself with his renewed interest in alchemy, and he produced no new works of great importance. Isaac became world famous not only among scientists, but to the general population. His book interested everyone from poets, to journalists, to teachers in every discipline.

Most people could not understand the high-level mathematics in Newton's book, but through simplified versions and word of mouth, the basic ideas contained in the *Principia* spread far and wide.

While one of the world's most celebrated and famous authors was hailed far and wide, he was mostly unable to enjoy his success. Isaac Newton was not well. For many years he had been working too hard, pushing himself to the limits of his endurance. Now, at the age of fifty-one, the years of strain were taking their toll.

Nobody really knows from what illness Newton suffered between 1693 and 1696. Some claimed that he had a nervous breakdown, others contend that he was simply physically exhausted. Whatever the cause, those years were later described by Isaac himself as "the black years." During this period, he achieved little in physics, made no real progress in alchemy, and suffered one bout of illness after another.

His friends rallied around him. Halley wrote frequently, as did others at the Royal Society and colleagues in London. All this support gradually helped him out of his black mood and physical sickness. But, the real turning point came in 1696, when he was made an offer that would change his life completely. He was invited to take up the important position of warden at the Royal Mint.

He accepted the offer immediately and began the next phase of his already remarkable life. For a while, he left scientific research altogether and launched himself into a new and prominent career as a high-ranking administrator in London.

"'The Scientific Revolution' was so important to the development of mankind that modern historians honour the phrase with initial capital letters. The new way of seeing the world that it introduced first tentatively surfaced with the publication of Copernicus's work in 1543. It reached its triumphal acceptance with the appearance in 1687 of Isaac Newton's *Principia*.

From *The History of Scientific Discovery*, edited by Jack Meadows

The stamping room in the Mint at the Tower of London. During Newton's time at the Mint, he made sweeping changes to the methods for purifying the metals used in the manufacture of coins.

The post at the Royal Mint was meant to be a reward for his scientific achievements and was primarily seen as a prestigious honorary title, with little actual responsibility. But Isaac Newton could never do anything half-heartedly. He threw himself into his new job with enormous energy, far exceeding the expectations of his superiors at the Treasury.

As it happened, the job came at an important time. England was changing its coinage, which had been badly affected by the civil war years. It was severely in need of updating and improving. Isaac supervised the pressing of the new coins and made sure that the money was distributed to the various banks around the country.

Clippers and Thieves

Another aspect of Isaac's job was to hunt down and
prosecute counterfeiters and a group of thieves
known as "clippers." These were people who
clipped off small pieces of coins, melted down the
metal, and extracted the silver.

Isaac applied all his cunning in tracking down
these criminals and bringing them to justice. He
was so successful, that within three years of his
appointment, he was made master of the Mint.

The Scientific Warden

Of all Isaac's responsibilities at the Royal Mint, the
most important was the essential task of testing the
purity of the coins. All the coins had to be of the

*Above is a Queen Anne
coin, one of those struck
under Newton's mastership.*

same weight, and each had to contain exactly the same quantity of precious metal. The job was not an easy one, but Isaac's strict scientific training proved useful once again.

Each day, he visited the pressing plant next to his offices. Using specially designed ladles, workmen would take out a small sample of the molten metal. It would then be taken back to the warden's laboratory where he conducted chemical experiments to make sure that the metal was of the required purity.

High Office

For years, Newton had paid little attention to research. He had kept his professorship at Cambridge until he was made master of the Royal Mint, but he no longer lectured and conducted very few experiments. The many demands of his new career were far too great.

The Royal Society was going through a disorganized time and there were many arguments among its leading members about the direction it should take. Isaac only attended meetings once in a while, partly because of his other interests, and partly because of the continuing arguments with his colleague Robert Hooke. In 1703, however, this longtime rival and antagonist died at the age of sixty-eight.

The members of the Royal Society voted to make Isaac Newton, their most famous and respected member, their new leader. In 1703, at the age of sixty, Isaac became president of the Royal Society.

Isaac worked hard to resolve the problems of the Society. For a number of years, the group had been presided over by leading politicians who were not interested in the Society's aims. The weekly meetings has gradually moved away from

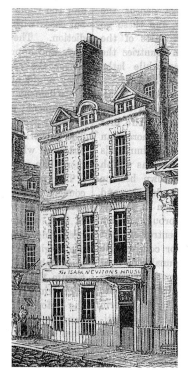

In becoming master of the Royal Mint, Isaac had established himself as a senior civil servant. He lived in a rather grand house near Leicester Square in London.

matters of scientific interest. When Newton took over as president, the membership was at an all time low. Having devoted his life to the Society's goals, Isaac was determined to revive interest in the organization. He devised a "scheme for establishing the Royal Society" to get it back on course again. In the "scheme," he said that the weekly meetings must provide serious discussion for the members and that only those with established and respected scientific reputations would be allowed to give demonstrations.

During Isaac's time as president, attendance at the meetings more than doubled. He managed to transform the membership from a small group of scientific colleagues to the world-famous and respected Society it is today.

A New Publication

Isaac was an internationally renowned scientist, master of the Royal Mint, and president of the Royal Society. The *Principia* was finding more and more enthusiastic readers every year, its strength growing in the eyes of scientists all over the world.

In 1704, only a few months after assuming the presidency at the Royal Society, Isaac was persuaded to publish the work he had begun when he was an undergraduate at Cambridge (his discoveries with light). This branch of physics is today called optics, and when he was finally ready to publish his studies in the spring of that year, he simply called his book *Opticks*. As people had expected, it was another runaway success.

The Final Years

The year after *Opticks* was published, Isaac Newton was knighted by Queen Anne for his great works in both science and public service. He was the first scientist ever to be honored in this way.

This picture, painted about 1690, shows the London of Isaac's time. Seen in the distance is the Tower of London, where Newton took up his position at the Mint in 1696.

Not everyone, however, loved England's most famous scientist. During this period Isaac had also made some new enemies. In his last years, as an old man in his late seventies, Isaac became involved in public arguments with two other famous scientists of the day. The worst of these debates was between Isaac and the German scientist, Gottfried Leibniz. Leibniz claimed that he, and not Newton, had invented the branch of mathematics known as calculus.

Isaac had used this new form of mathematics to solve complicated problems nearly sixty years earlier when he was first developing his notions of mechanics and optics, but the issue had only just come to Leibniz's attention, prompted by its use in the world-famous *Opticks*.

Leibniz did not really have a chance against his opponent's power and influence. Isaac Newton was the greatest scientist in the world, leader of the most successful and respected scientific society on earth, and a knight.

Isaac again won the public argument by persuading his colleagues that Leibniz had first seen the calculus in his early publications and had copied the idea from him. In this way, he obtained the agreement of the scientific world that he, and not Leibniz was the first to formulate calculus. Although Leibniz is remembered for his contributions to the field of calculus—and for many other branches of physics in which he worked—he died without the riches, power, or recognition that were bestowed upon his famous British rival.

Fortunate Newton, happy childhood of science! He who has time and tranquility, can by reading this book live again the wonderful events which the great Newton experienced in his young days. Nature to him was an open book, whose letters he could read without effort.

Albert Einstein, from the foreword to the 1931 edition of *Optics*

Newton's Legacy

Sir Isaac Newton died on March 20, 1727, at age eighty-four. He had been ill and bedridden for several months. He was buried on April 4 among Britain's kings and queens, dukes and earls, in London's Westminster Abbey.

He had become so highly regarded during his life, that for a week before the funeral, he had lain in state in the Abbey. This was a mark of respect usually reserved only for monarchs. At the funeral, Newton's coffin was carried by two dukes, three earls, and the Lord Chancellor.

It is hard to exaggerate Sir Isaac Newton's contribution to science. As a man, he was often a difficult and argumentative genius who could not tolerate being contradicted. He fought fiercely with his rivals and managed always to win. There were many who disliked him.

Many never forgave him for what they felt was unfair treatment of his fellow scientists. His critics claimed that Isaac did not give others due credit for their work. They implied that Isaac had enjoyed sending criminals to their death while at the Royal Mint, and suggested that he had manipulated influential people in order to succeed. All of these accusations may have been founded in truth, but many other people have said that Isaac Newton was a generous man who often helped poor families. It is a fact that he gave large sums to charity, and never failed to provide financial help to distant relatives in troubled times.

The greatest scientist had grown increasingly eccentric in his old age. He had become obsessed with having his portrait painted, and insisted on a new one every two or three years (this accounts for the unusually large number of well-painted portraits of the elderly Newton, which have survived to the present day).

"He has become for me ... one of the tiny handful of supreme geniuses who have shaped the categories of the human intellect."

Richard Westfall, from his biography, *Never at Rest*

"I don't know what I may seem to the world, but, as to myself, I seem to have been only like a boy playing on the sea shore, and diverting myself in now and then finding a smoother pebble or a prettier shell than ordinary whilst the great ocean of truth lay all undiscovered before me."

Isaac Newton

Many paintings and sculptures of Newton were made during the great man's lifetime and after his death in 1727. This marble sculpture, by Louis Francis Roubilliac, can be found today in the antechapel of Trinity College, Cambridge.

He never married and had no heirs. His rather valuable estate was taken over by descendants of his stepfather, Barnabas Smith. But Isaac left far more to the world than simple property. He created an entirely new approach to science and an original way of solving many of its most fundamental problems.

Today, more than 350 years after his birth, scientists from around the world—in all areas of study—still use the very same principles and ideas that were first laid down by this extraordinary man.

Important Dates

1642	**Aug:** The English civil war breaks out and continues until 1649. **Dec. 25:** Newton is born in Woolsthorpe, England, to Hannah Newton. His father had died three months earlier.
1655	Newton, age twelve, starts at Grantham grammar school.
1661	**June:** Newton, age eighteen, enters Cambridge University.
1664	**Spring:** Newton, age twenty-one, begins his experiments with light.
1665	Newton becomes a Bachelor of Arts and begins to develop his own advanced mathematics. The Great Plague breaks out in London and spreads to other cities. Newton leaves Cambridge and returns to Woolsthorpe.
1666	Isaac Newton makes great breakthroughs in understanding the laws of gravity. **Sept. 2-6:** The Great Fire of London.
1667	**Mar:** Isaac Newton returns to Cambridge University. Within six months, he is elected Fellow of Trinity College.
1669	**July:** Isaac Newton's work, *De Analysis*, is circulated. **Oct:** Isaac Newton is appointed Lucasian Professor of Mathematics at Cambridge University. Age twenty-six, he is the youngest ever to hold the post.
1670–1	Isaac Newton develops his reflecting telescope.
1672	Isaac Newton is invited to join the Royal Society, a group of senior scientists. **Feb:** Newton delivers his first paper to the Society.
1679	**June:** Isaac Newton's mother, Hannah, dies.
1684	Isaac Newton begins work on his book, *Philosophiae Naturalis Principia Mathematica*, usually referred to as the *Principia*.
1689	Isaac Newton is elected to represent Cambridge University in the "Convention Parliament."
1693–96	Isaac Newton suffers from mystery illness.
1696	**Mar:** Recovered from his illness, Isaac Newton accepts the position of Warden of the Royal Mint
1699	**Dec:** Aged 47, Isaac Newton is made Master of the Royal Mint.
1701	Isaac Newton is elected Member of Parliament for Cambridge University.
1703	**Nov. 30:** Isaac Newton is elected President of the Royal Society.
1704	Newton's book on his discoveries with light, *Optics*, is published.
1705	Isaac Newton is knighted by Queen Anne. He is the first scientist to receive the award.
1727	**Mar 20:** Sir Isaac Newton, age eighty-four, dies.

Scientific Terms

Astronomy The scientific study of the heavenly bodies, particularly their movements, positions, composition, and distribution.

Biology The science of life and living organisms, covering the study of their structure, function, growth, origin, ecology, and evolution.

Calculus The branch of mathematics that allows continuously varying quantities to be manipulated.

Centrifugal force The apparent tendency of a spinning body to move outward from the middle of its axis of rotation.

Combustion A chemical reaction in which a substance is mixed, usually with oxygen and produces heat, light, and flame.

Condenser In chemistry, an apparatus for changing a substance in its gaseous state into a liquid.

Force An influence that is capable of changing a body's state of rest or uniform motion in a straight line.

Formula In mathematics and physics, a statement or law expressed using symbols. In chemistry, symbols that represent the composition of a substance.

Friction A force that resists the movement of one surface against another with which it is in contact.

Geometry The branch of mathematics concerned with the properties, measurement, and relationship of lines, points, angles, surfaces, and solids.

Gravity The force of attraction exerted by Earth, or another planet or satellite, on bodies on or near its surface.

Laser (Light Amplification by Stimulated Emission of Radiation) A device that produces a narrow, powerful, highly directional beam of light.

Mass The amount of material in an object.

Mechanics The branch of physics concerned with the study of moving objects and the forces acting upon them.

Optics The scientific study of light and vision.

Prism In optics, a triangular block of glass or plastic used to disperse light or to change its direction.

Spectrum The rainbow-effect produced when a beam of light is passed through a prism.

Spectroscopy The study of the spectrum.

Theorem In mathematics, a rule usually expressed as a formula.

Velocity The speed at which an object travels in a particular direction.

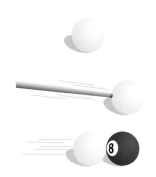

Newton's Laws of Motion

1. Every body continues in a state of rest or uniform motion in a straight line unless it is acted on by an external force.
2. When a force acts on a body, the rate of change of momentum of the body is proportional to the force and changes in the direction in which the force acts.
3. To every action there is an equal and opposite reaction.

Newton's Law of Gravitation

All bodies in the universe attract each other with a force that is directly proportional to the product of the masses of the bodies and inversely proportional to the square of the distance between them.

For More Information

Books

Anderson, Margaret Jean. *Isaac Newton: The Greatest Scientist of All Time* (Great Minds of Science). Springfield, NJ: Enslow Publishers, 1996.

Jeffries, Michael. Gary Lewis (Contributor). *Inventors and Inventions*. New York, NY: Smithmark Publishers, 1996.

Lyon, Sue. Paul Berman. Keith Wicks. *Experiments in Physics* (Science in Action). Tarrytown, NY: Benchmark Books, 1993.

Oxlade, Chris. Andrew Farmer (Illustrator). Julia Pearson (Illustrator). *Energy and Movement* (Step-By-Step Science). Danbury, CT: Children's Press, 1999.

White, Larry. Laurie Hamilton (Illustrator). *Gravity: Simple Experiments for Young Scientists*. Danbury, CT: Millbrook Press, 1995.

Wilkinson, Philip. Michael Pollard. Robert Ingpen (Illustrator). *Scientists Who Changed the World* (Turning Points in History). New York, NY: Chelsea House, 1994.

Web Sites

Sir Isaac Newton
Find photographs of places where Newton lived and worked, biographical information, and information on the scientist's publications—www.newtonia.freeserve.co.uk.

Hubble Space Telescope's Greatest Hits
Check out the gallery of amazing photographs featuring celestial objects seen through this extraordinary telescope—oposite.stsci.edu/pubinfo/BestofHST95.html.

NASA
Learn all about the latest space missions, Earth and space science, launches, astronauts, and much more—www.nasa.gov.

Index